HAL LEONARD SOLO GUITAR LIBRARY

FINGERSTYLE GREATS PLAY
POP/ROCK HITS

T0085656

2 AND SO IT GOES
Tommy Emmanuel

6 BLUEBERRY HILL
John Renbourn

11 CRAZY
Don Ross

15 EVERYBODY WANTS
TO RULE THE WORLD
Andy McKee

22 HEY JUDE
Chris Proctor

27 LITTLE MARTHA
Leo Kottke

30 SEA OF LOVE
John Fahey

33 SPIRITS IN
THE MATERIAL WORLD
Antoine Dufuor

36 SUPERSTITION
Pete Huttlinger

41 A WHITER SHADE OF PALE
Stephen Bennett

46 Guitar Notation Legend

Music transcriptions by Pete Billmann and David Stocker

ISBN 978-1-4803-1292-0

HAL•LEONARD®
CORPORATION

7777 W. BLUEMOUND RD. P.O. BOX 13819 MILWAUKEE, WI 53213

For all works contained herein:
Unauthorized copying, arranging, adapting, recording, Internet posting, public performance,
or other distribution of the printed music in this publication is an infringement of copyright.
Infringers are liable under the law.

Visit Hal Leonard Online at
www.halleonard.com

And So It Goes

Words and Music by Billy Joel

Capo IV

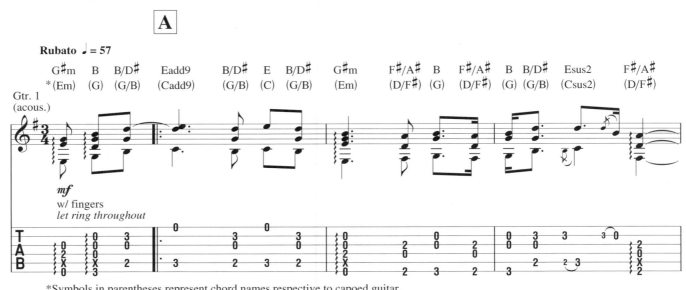

*Symbols in parentheses represent chord names respective to capoed guitar.
Symbols above reflect actual sounding chords. Capoed fret is "0" in tab.

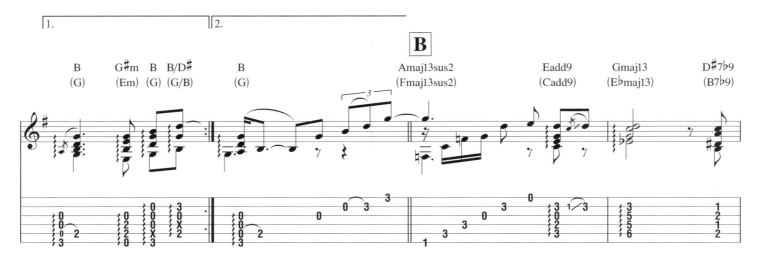

Copyright © 1989 JOELSONGS
This arrangement Copyright © 2013 JOELSONGS
All Rights Administered by ALMO MUSIC CORP.
All Rights Reserved   Used by Permission

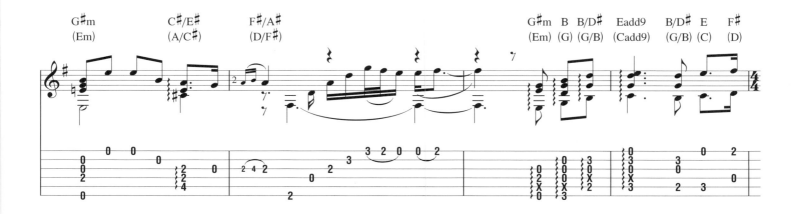

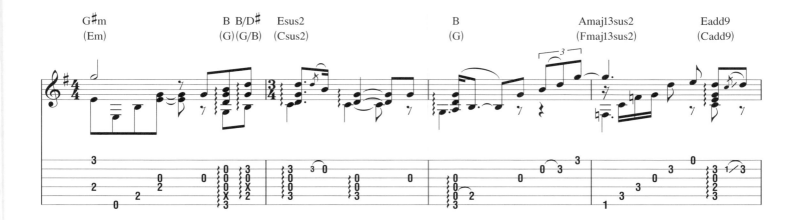

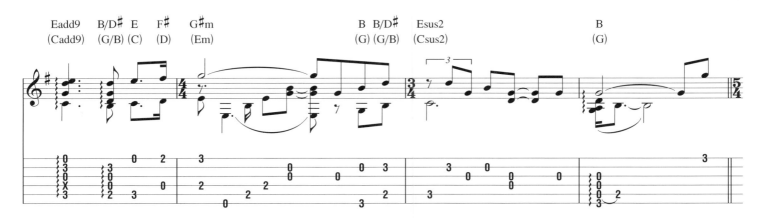

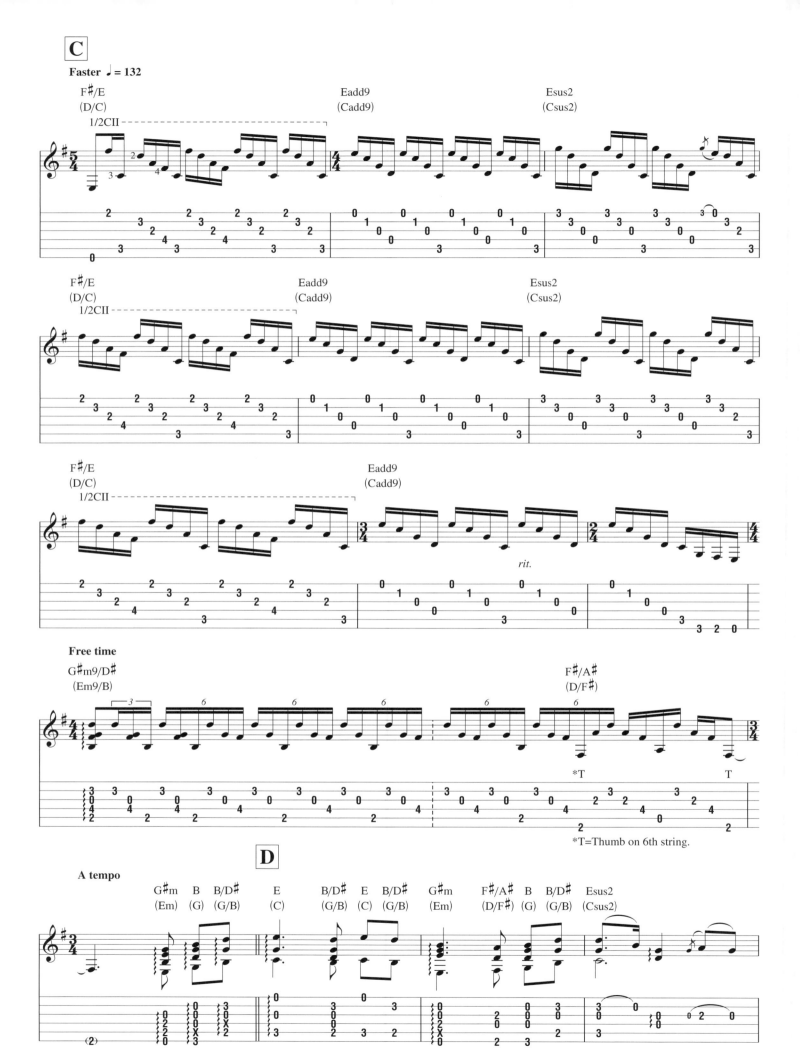

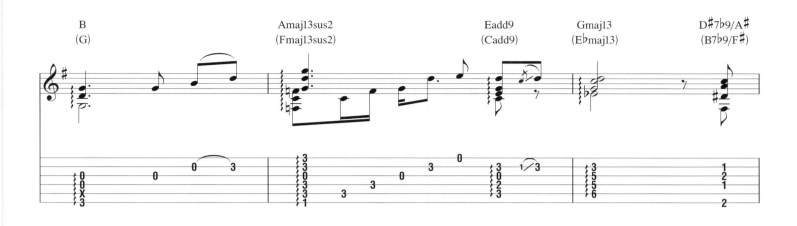

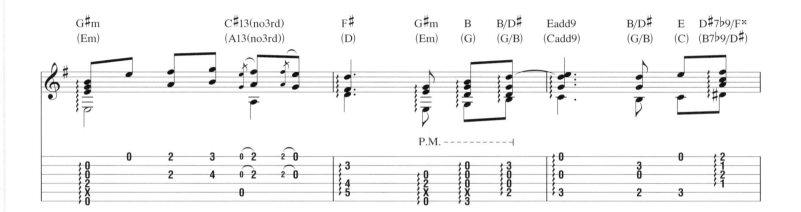

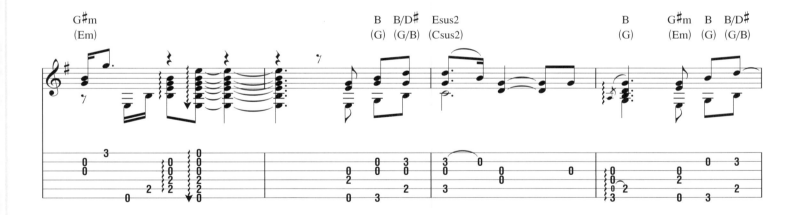

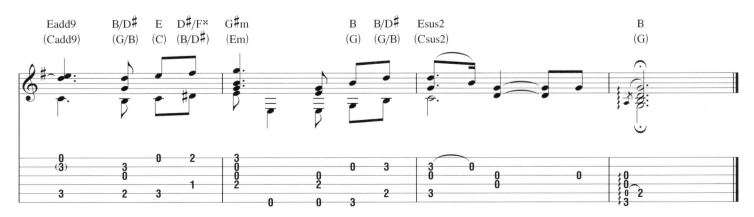

from John Renbourn - *Palermo Snow*

Blueberry Hill

Words and Music by Al Lewis, Larry Stock and Vincent Rose

Open G tuning:
(low to high) D-G-D-G-B-D

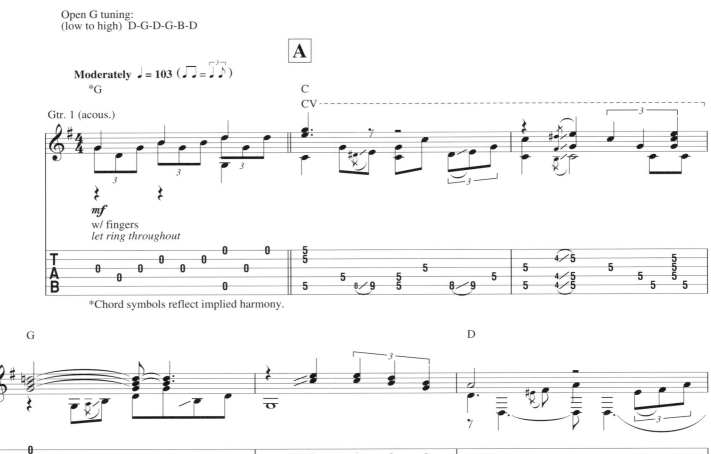

*Chord symbols reflect implied harmony.

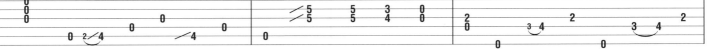

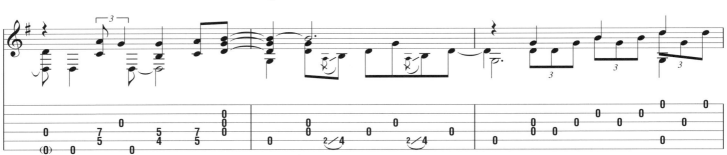

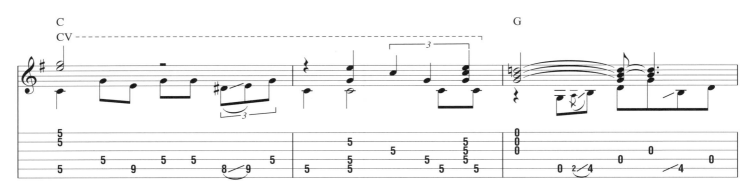

Copyright © 1940 by Chappell & Co.
Copyright Renewed, Assigned to Chappell & Co., Larry Stock Music Co. and Sovereign Music Corp.
This arrangement Copyright © 2013 by Chappell & Co., Larry Stock Music Co. and Sovereign Music Corp.
All Rights for Larry Stock Music Co. Administered by Larry Spier, Inc., New York
International Copyright Secured   All Rights Reserved

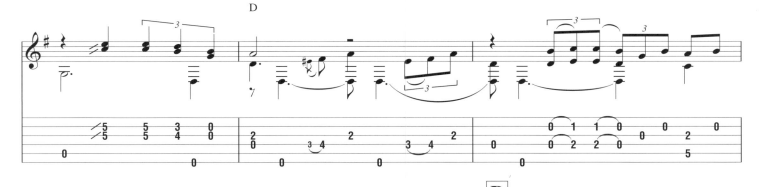

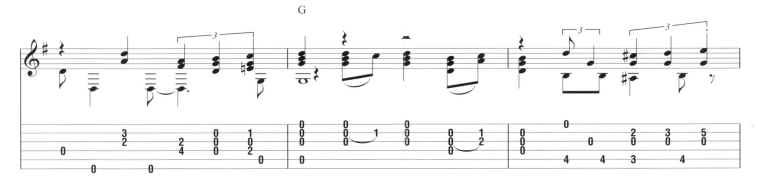

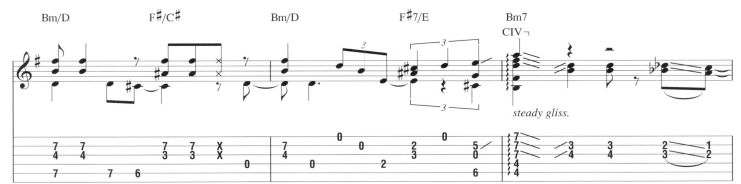

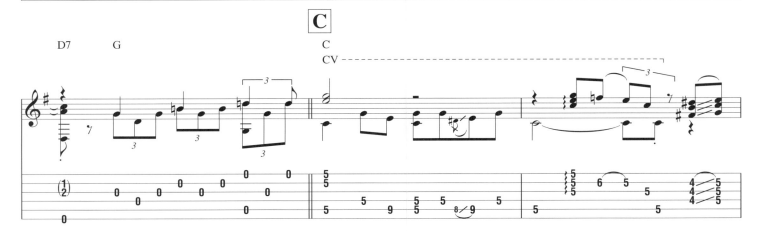

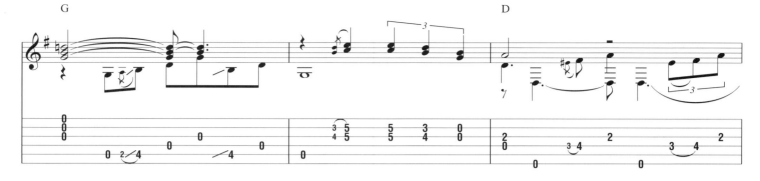

D

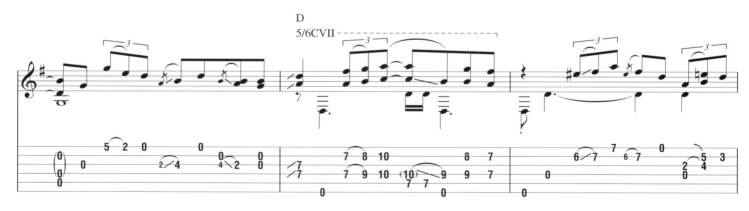

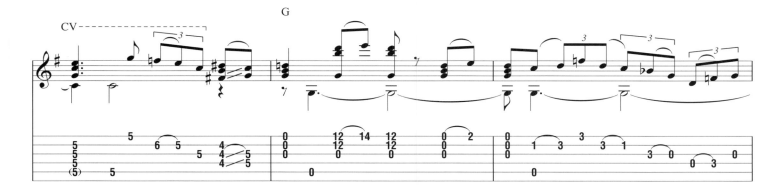

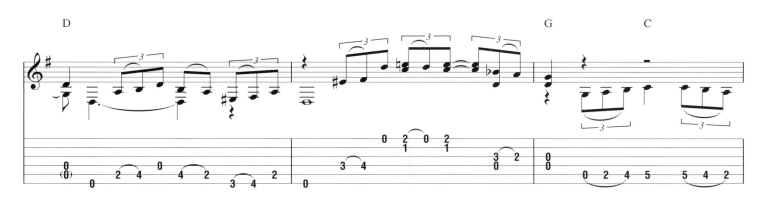

E

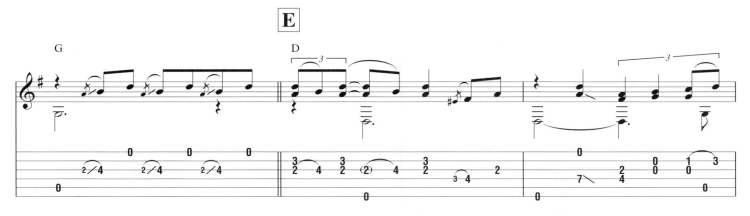

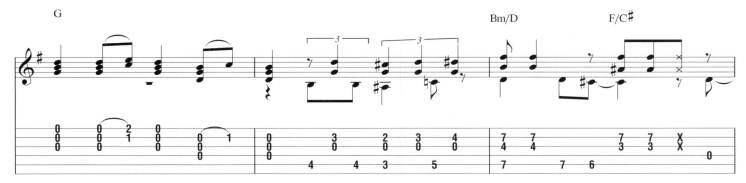

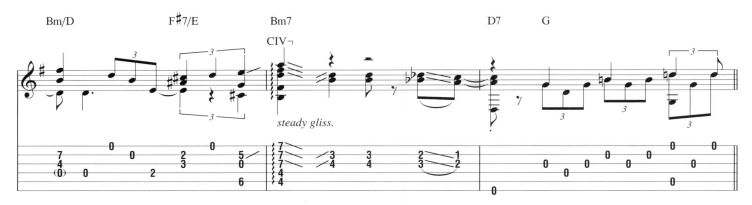

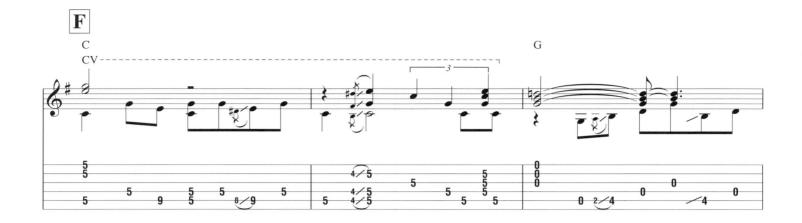

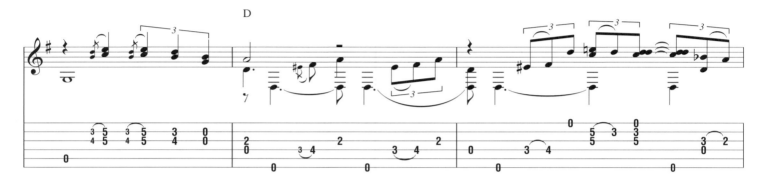

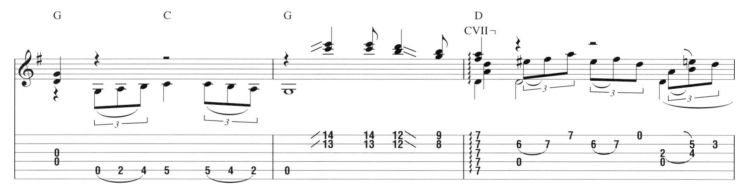

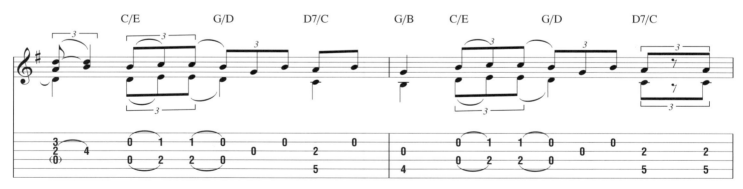

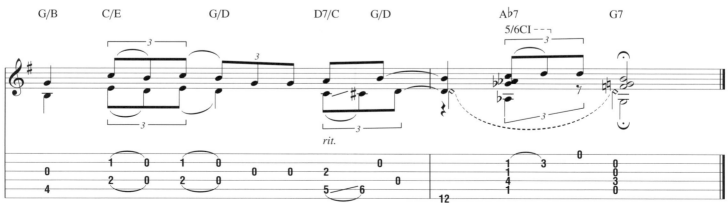

Crazy

Tuning:
(low to high) C-G-C-G-B♭-C

**Words and Music by Brian Burton, Thomas Callaway,
GianPiero Reverberi and GianFranco Reverberi**

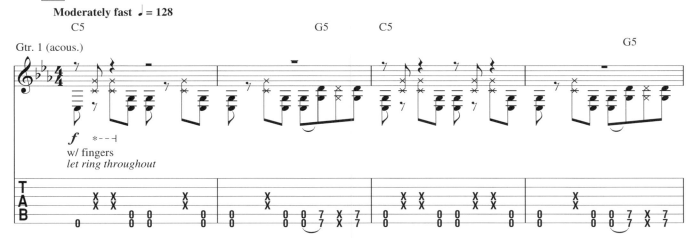

*Upstemmed x's indicate L.H. slap; downstemmed x's indicate R.H. slap.

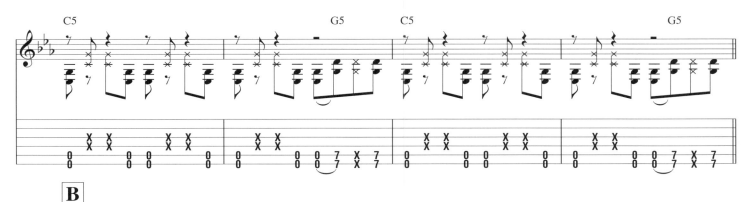

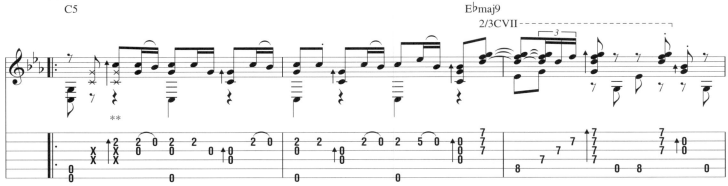

**Strum w/ back of R.H. nails.

Copyright © 2006 Chrysalis Music Ltd., Warner/Chappell Music Publishing Ltd. and Universal Music Publishing Ricordi Srl
This arrangement Copyright © 2013 Chrysalis Music Ltd., Warner/Chappell Music Publishing Ltd. and Universal Music Publishing Ricordi Srl
All Rights for Chrysalis Music Ltd. Administered by Chrysalis Music Group Inc., a BMG Chrysalis company
All Rights for Warner/Chappell Music Publishing Ltd. in the U.S. and Canada Administered by Warner-Tamerlane Publishing Corp.
All Rights for Universal Music Publishing Ricordi Srl in the U.S. and Canada Administered by Killer Tracks
All Rights Reserved Used by Permission
- contains a sample of "Last Men Standing" by GianPiero Reverberi and GianFranco Reverberi

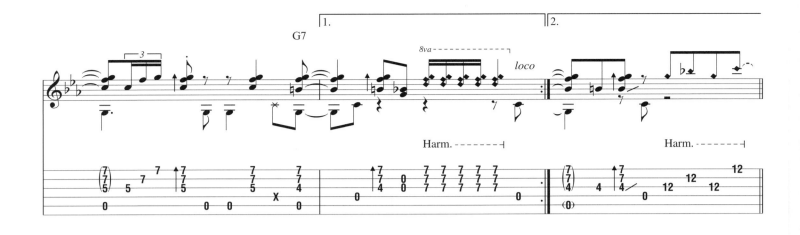

% **C**

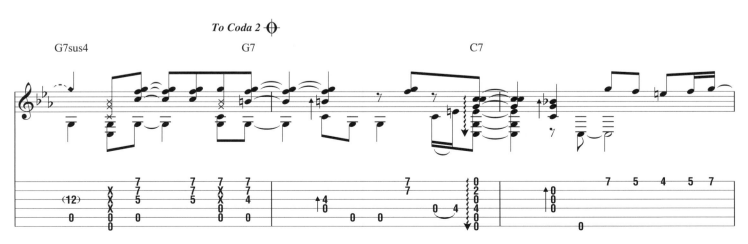

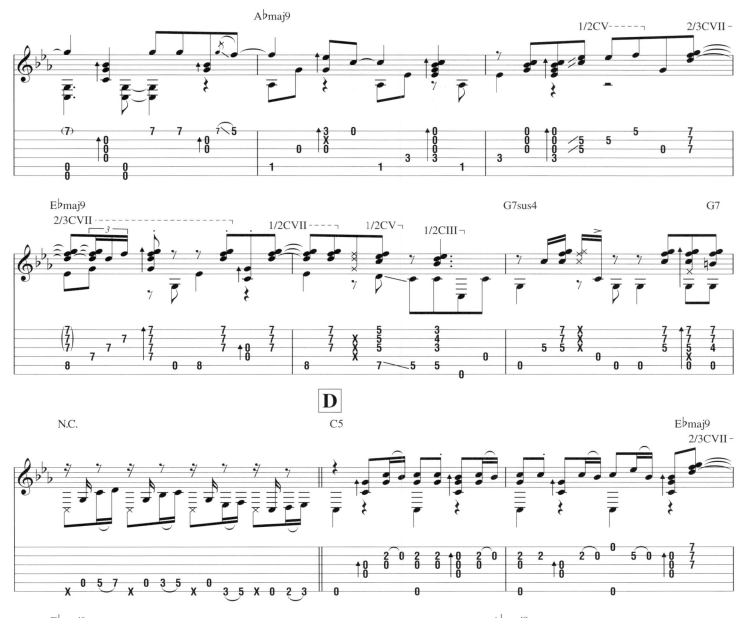

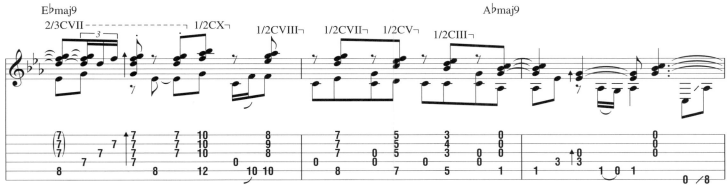

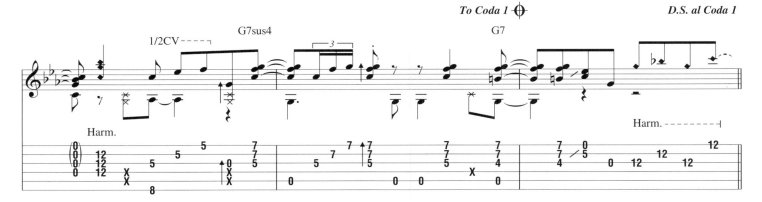

E

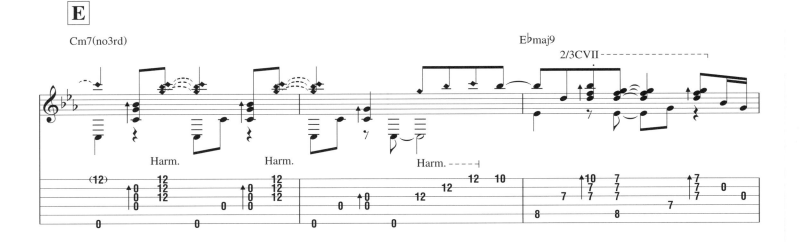

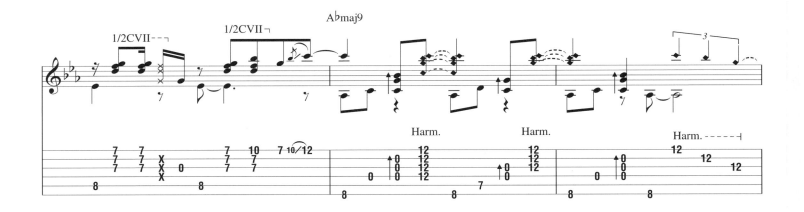

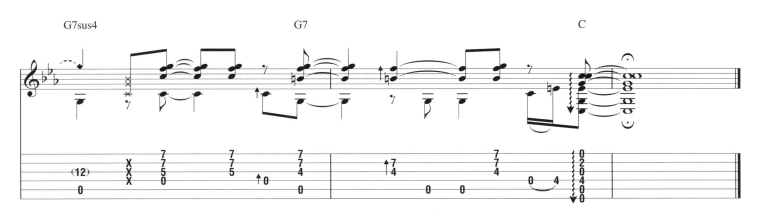

from Andy McKee - *Joyland*

Everybody Wants to Rule the World

Words and Music by Ian Stanley, Roland Orzabal and Chris Hughes

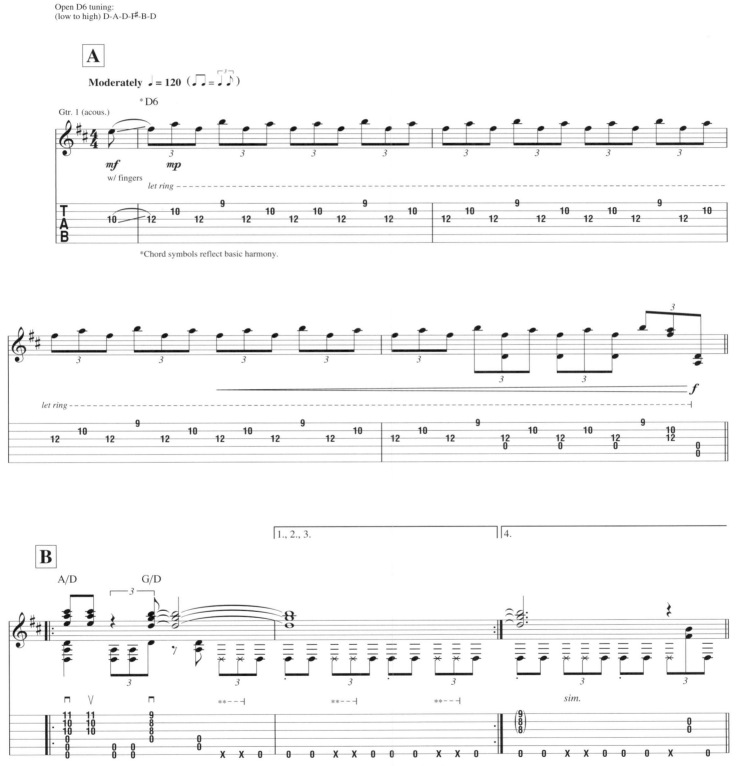

*Chord symbols reflect basic harmony.

**Slap all strings w/ pick hand when low D X is written throughout.

© 1985 EMI VIRGIN MUSIC LTD., EMI 10 MUSIC LTD. and AMUSEMENTS LTD.
This arrangement © 2013 EMI VIRGIN MUSIC LTD., EMI 10 MUSIC LTD. and AMUSEMENTS LTD.
All Rights in the U.S. and Canada Controlled and Administered by EMI VIRGIN SONGS, INC.
All Rights in the world excluding the U.S. and Canada Controlled and Administered by EMI VIRGIN MUSIC LTD.
All Rights Reserved   International Copyright Secured   Used by Permission

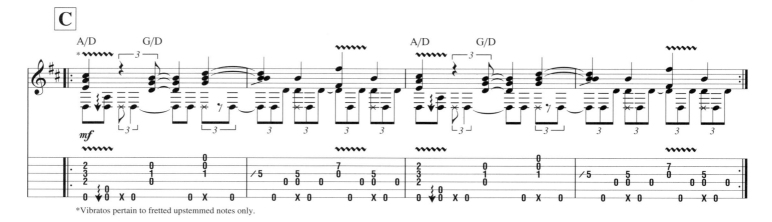

*Vibratos pertain to fretted upstemmed notes only.

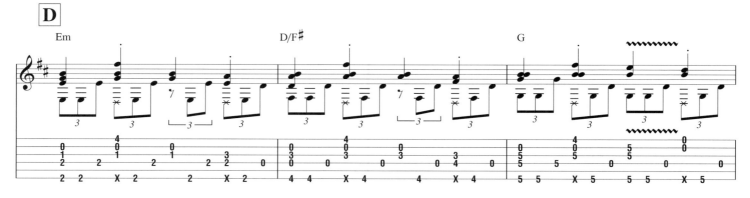

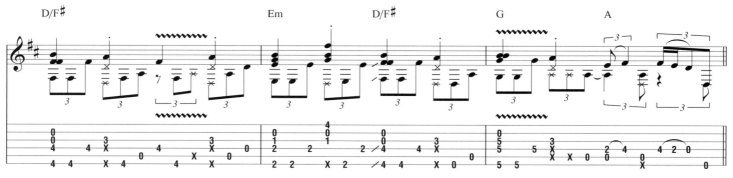

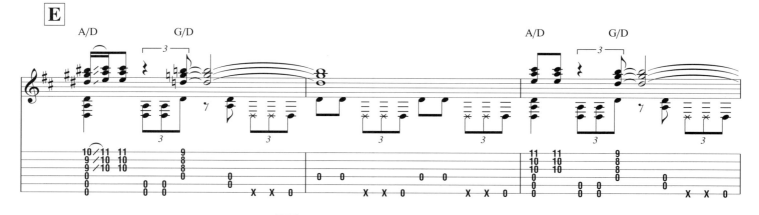

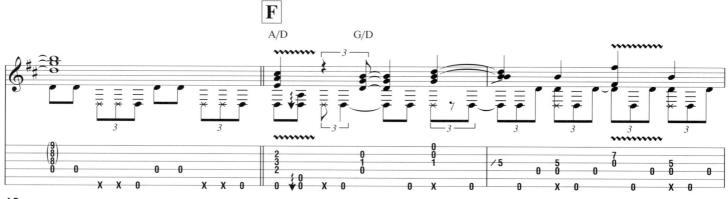

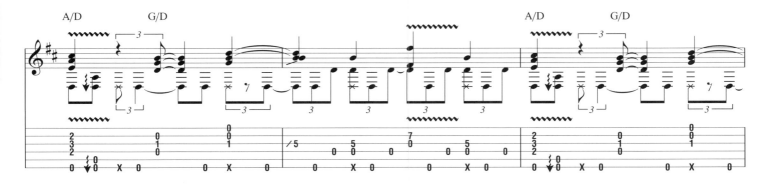

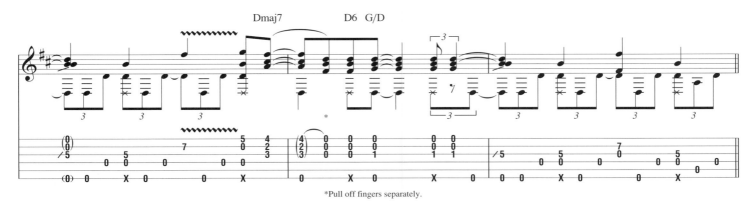

*Pull off fingers separately.

G

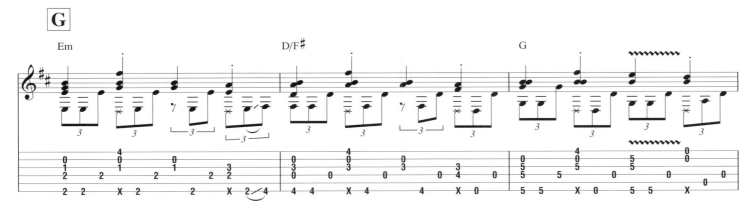

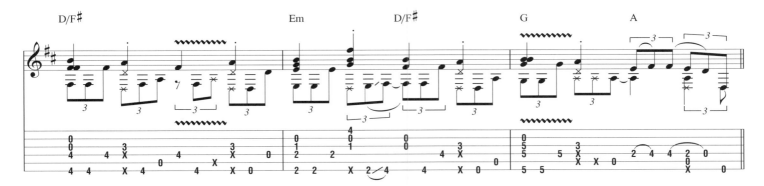

H

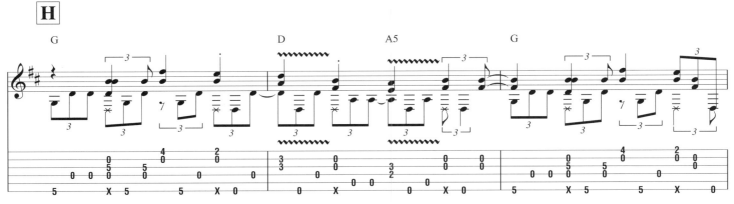

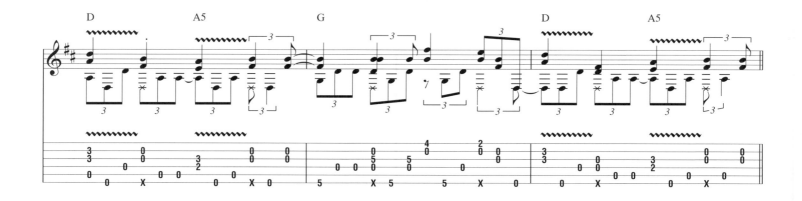

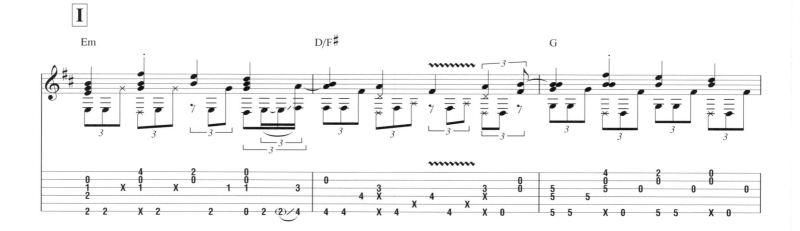

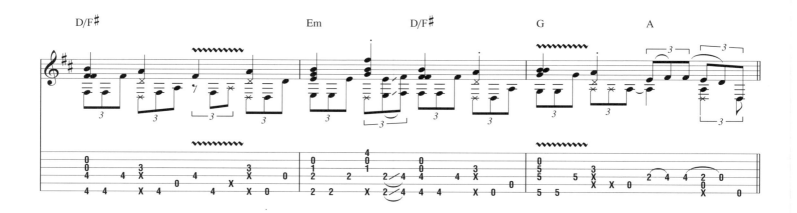

I

J

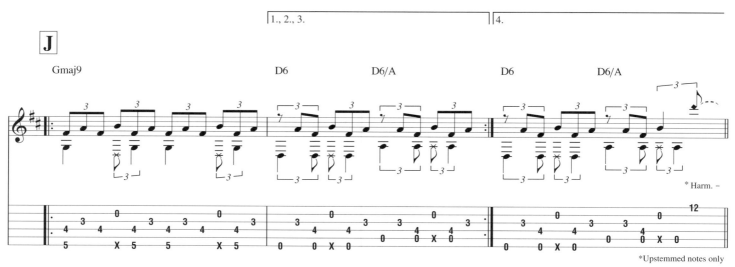

*Upstemmed notes only

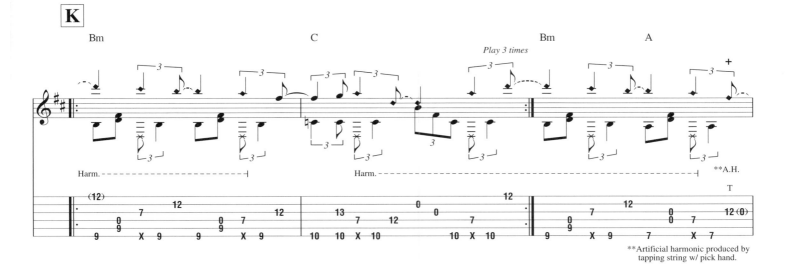

Play 3 times

**A.H.

Harm.

**Artificial harmonic produced by
tapping string w/ pick hand.

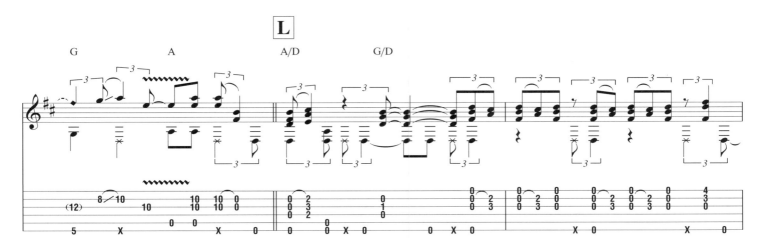

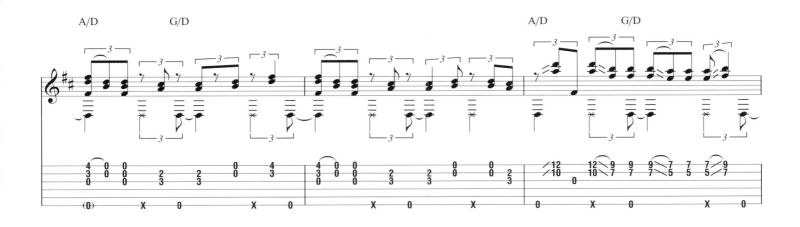

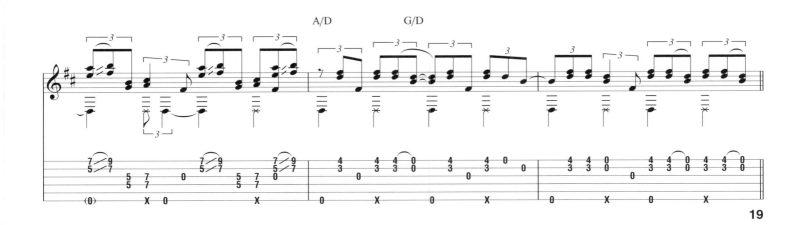

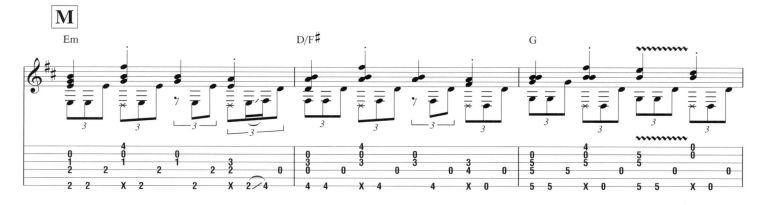

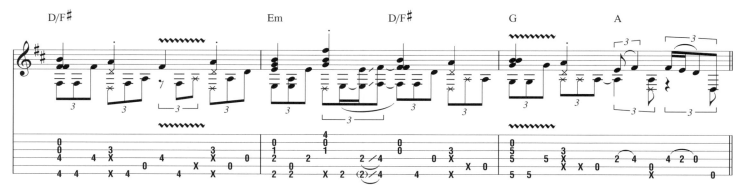

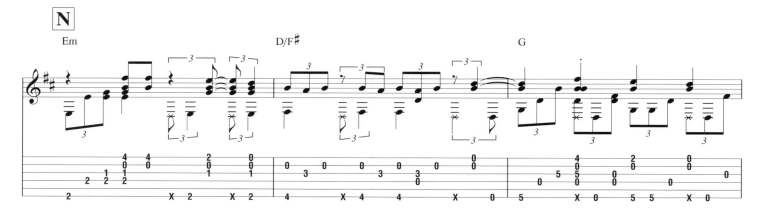

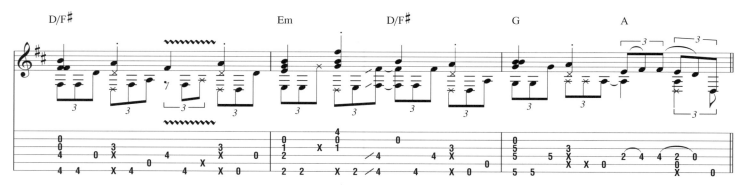

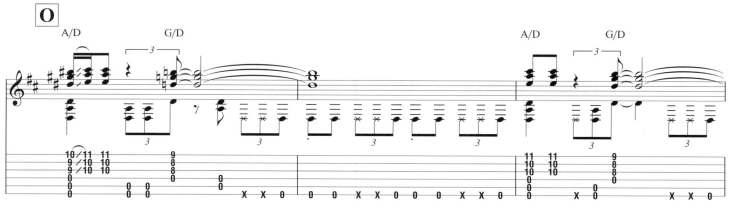

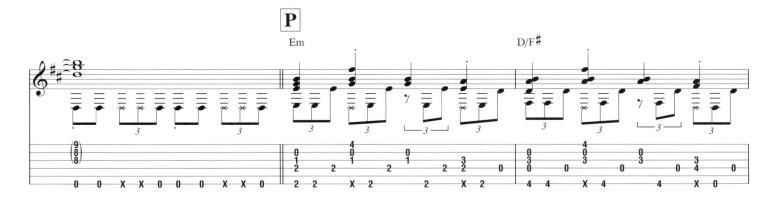

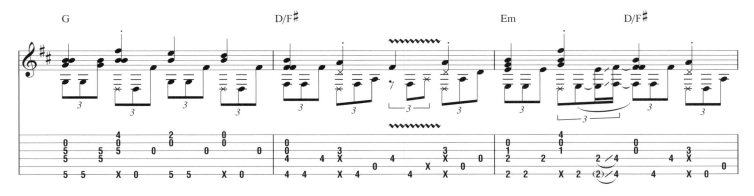

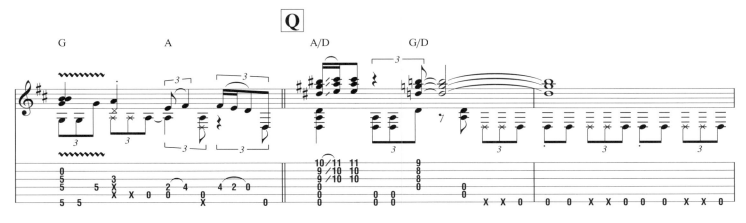

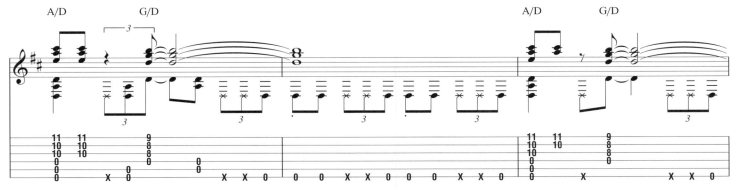

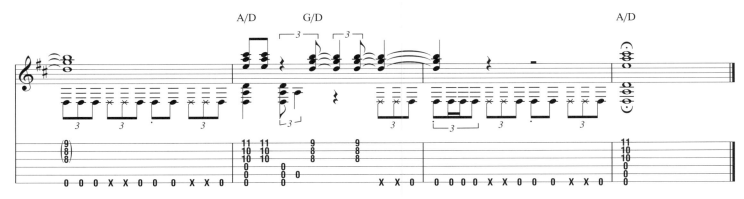

from Chris Proctor - *Under the Influence*

Hey Jude

Words and Music by John Lennon and Paul McCartney

Tuning:
(low to high) C-G-D-G-A-D

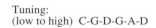

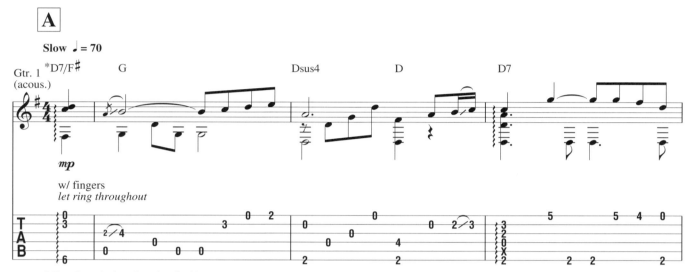

*Chord symbols reflect implied harmony.

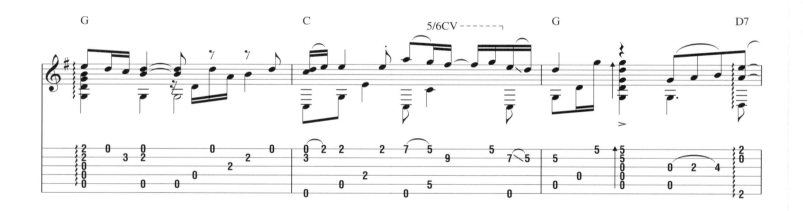

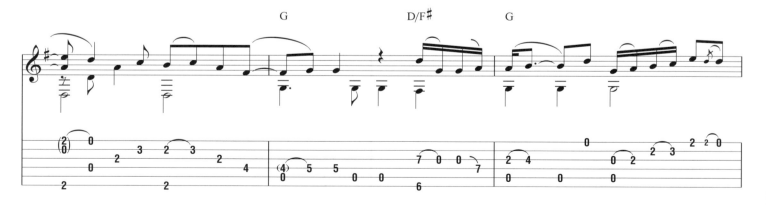

Copyright © 1968 Sony/ATV Music Publishing LLC
Copyright Renewed
This arrangement Copyright © 2013 Sony/ATV Music Publishing LLC
All Rights Administered by Sony/ATV Music Publishing LLC, 8 Music Square West, Nashville, TN 37203
International Copyright Secured   All Rights Reserved

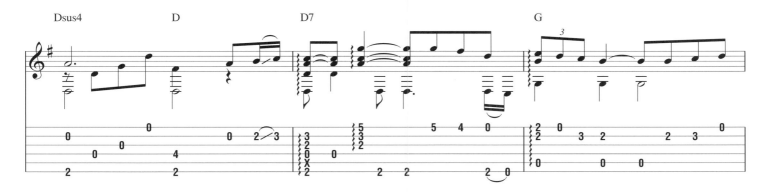

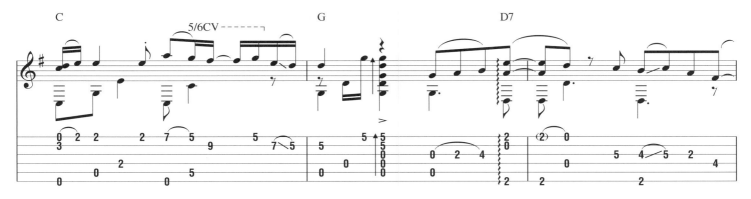

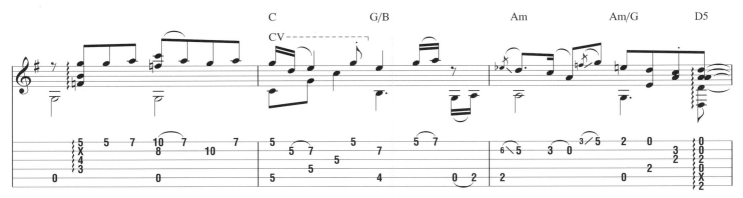

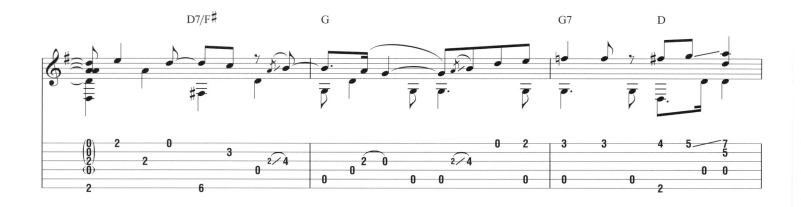

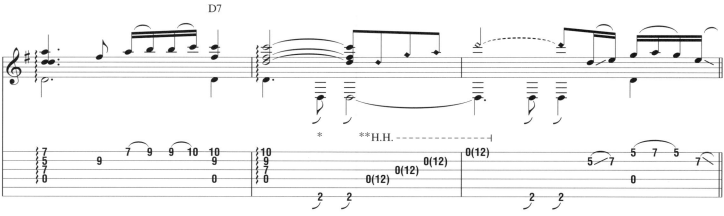

*Hammer onto 6th str. w/ pick-hand index finger while holding chord.
**While holding the bass note with your pick hand, perform harp harmonic w/ fret hand.

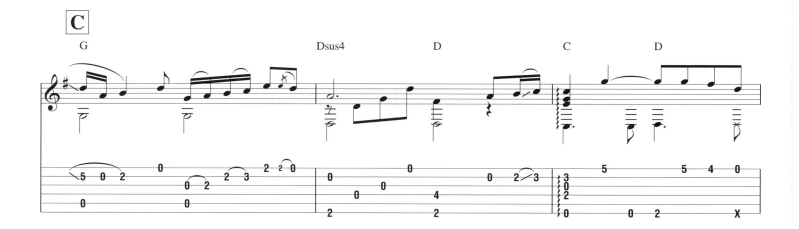

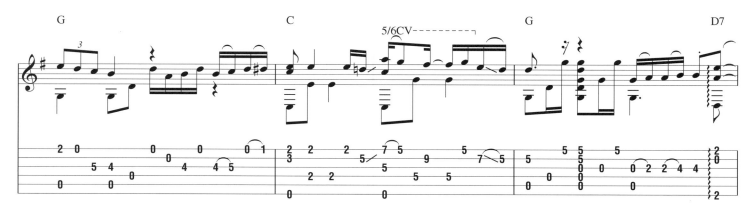

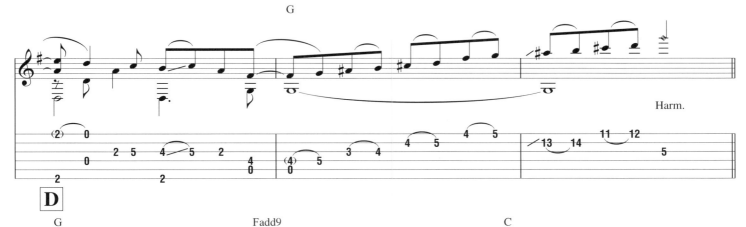

D

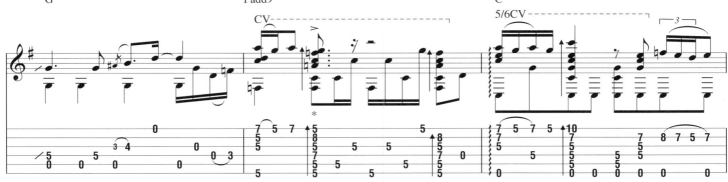

*Strum w/ back of pick-hand nails.

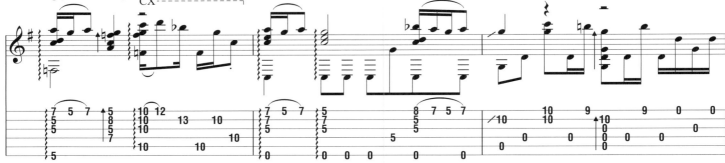

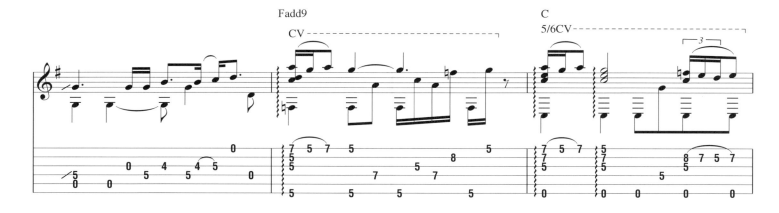

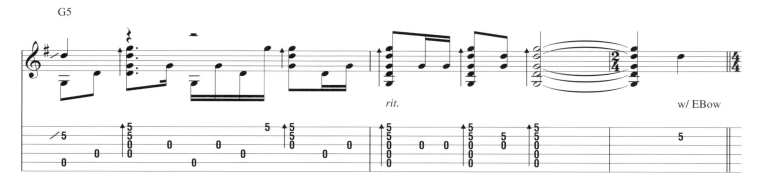

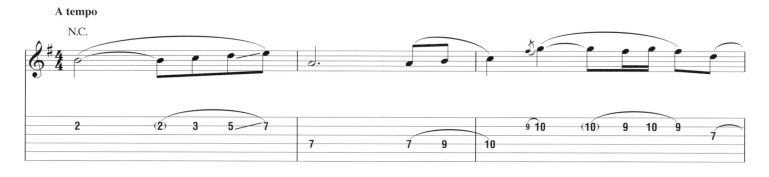

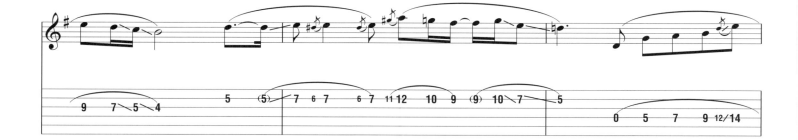

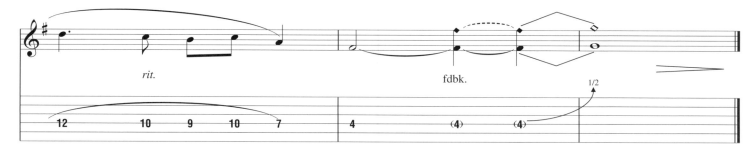

from Leo Kottke - *A Shout Toward Noon*

Little Martha

Written by Duane Allman

Open D tuning, down 1/2 step:
(low to high) Db-Ab-Db-F-Ab-Db

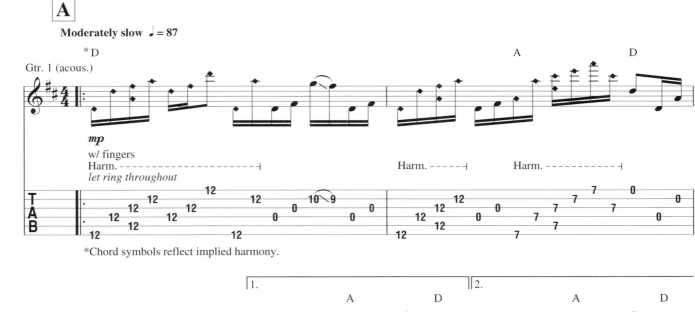

*Chord symbols reflect implied harmony.

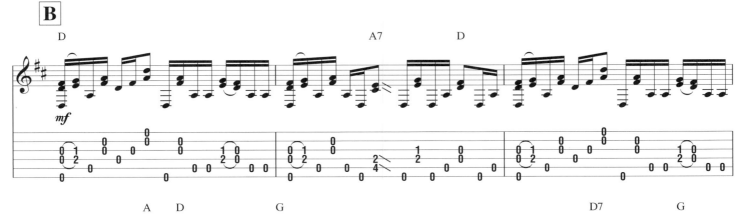

© 1972 (Renewed 2000) HAPPILY MARRIED MUSIC (BMI)
This arrangement © 2013 HAPPILY MARRIED MUSIC (BMI)
All Rights Controlled and Administered by BUG MUSIC, INC., A BMG CHRYSALIS COMPANY
All Rights Reserved   Used by Permission

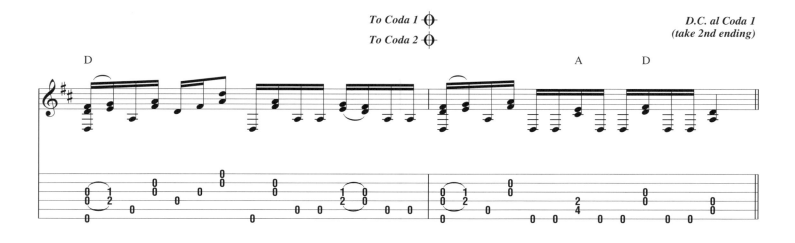

⊕ **Coda 1**

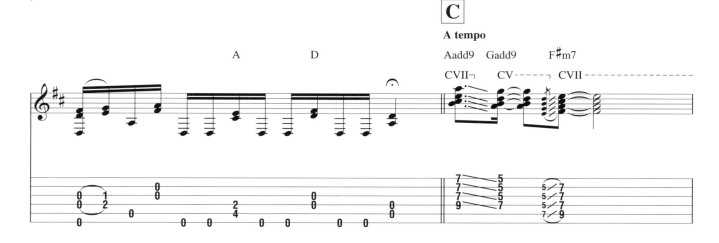

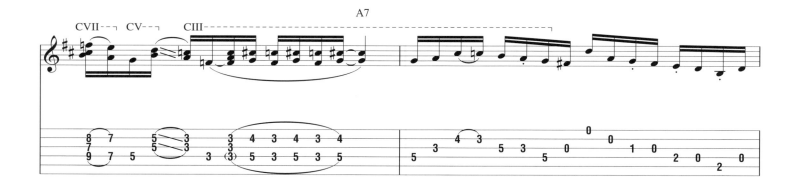

D.C. al Coda 2
(take 2nd ending)

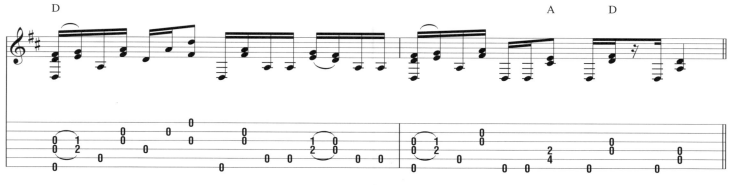

D

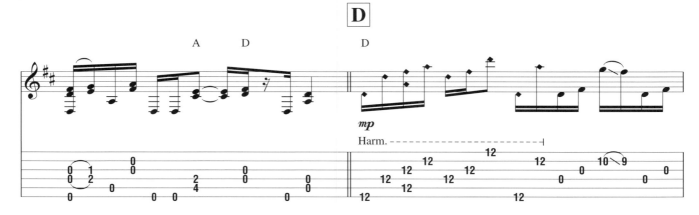

E

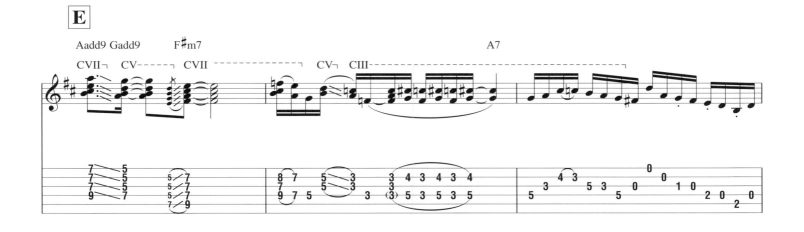

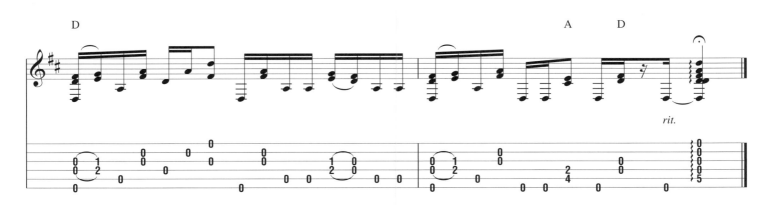

Sea of Love

Words and Music by George Khoury and Philip Baptiste

Open G tuning, capo I:
(low to high) D-G-D-G-B-D

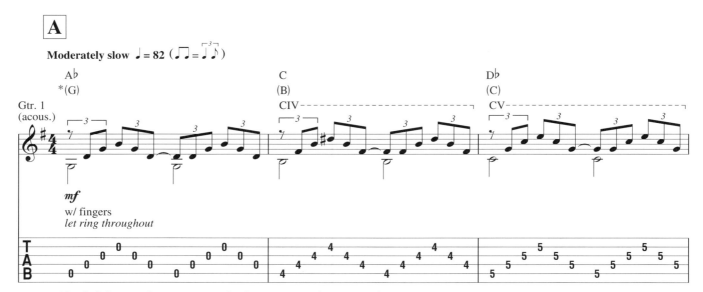

*Symbols in parentheses represent chord names respective to capoed gtr.
Symbols above reflect actual sounding chords. Capoed fret is "0" in tab.
Chord symbols reflect implied harmony.

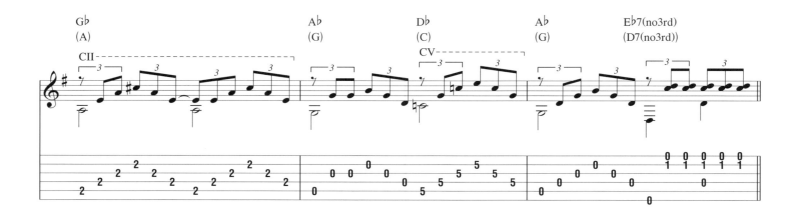

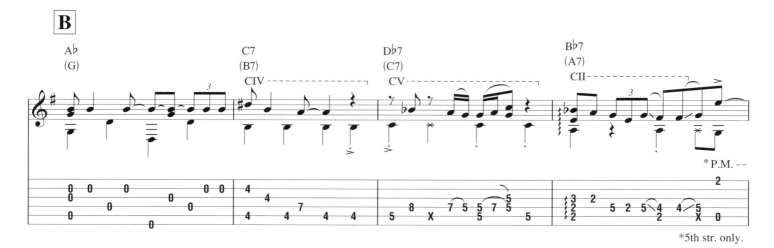

*5th str. only.

Copyright © 1957, 1959 by Fort Knox Music Inc., Trio Music Company and Tek Publishing
Copyright Renewed
This arrangement Copyright © 2013 by Fort Knox Music Inc., Trio Music Company and Tek Publishing
All Rights for Trio Music Company Administered by BUG Music Inc., a BMG Chrysalis company
International Copyright Secured   All Rights Reserved
Used by Permission

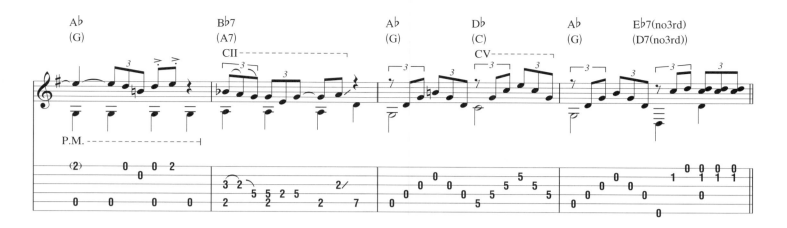

C

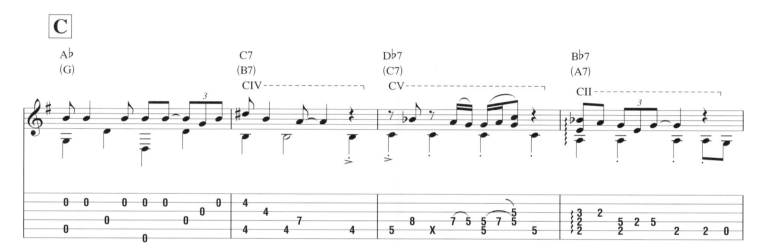

D

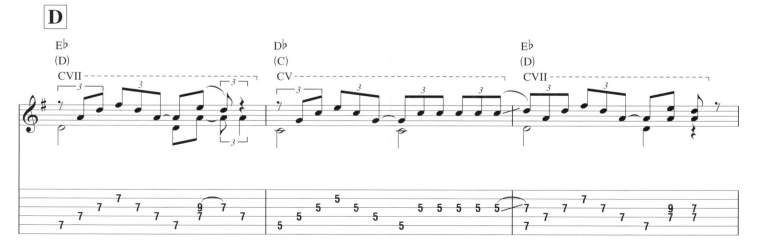

from Antoine Dufour - *Convergences*

Spirits in the Material World

Music and Lyrics by Sting

Tuning:
(low to high) E-A-C-G-B-E

A

Moderately ♩ = 119

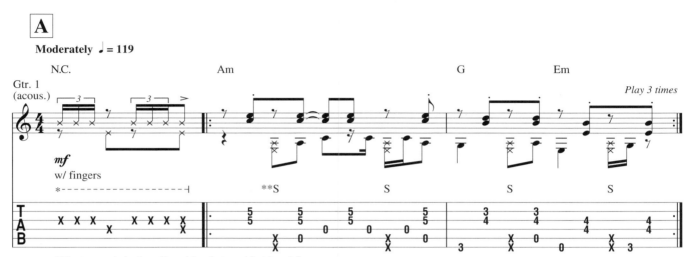

*Upstemmed rhythm: Tap side of gtr. w/ fret-hand fingers.
Downstemmed rhythm: tap top of gtr. w/ pick-hand palm.

**Slap 5th & 6th strings w/ pick-hand thumb.

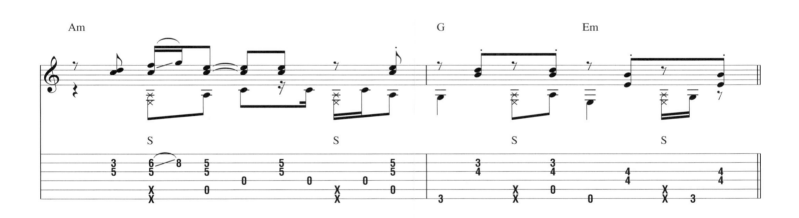

B

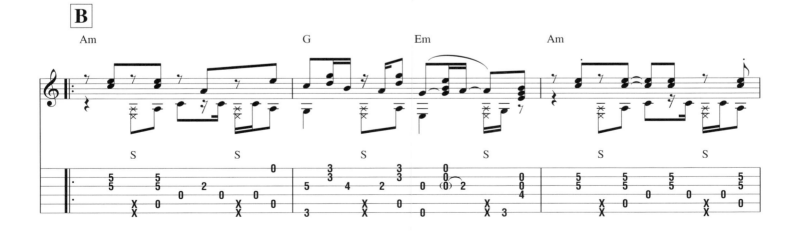

© 1981 G.M. SUMNER
This arrangement © 2013 G.M. SUMNER
Administered by EMI MUSIC PUBLISHING LIMITED
All Rights Reserved   International Copyright Secured   Used by Permission

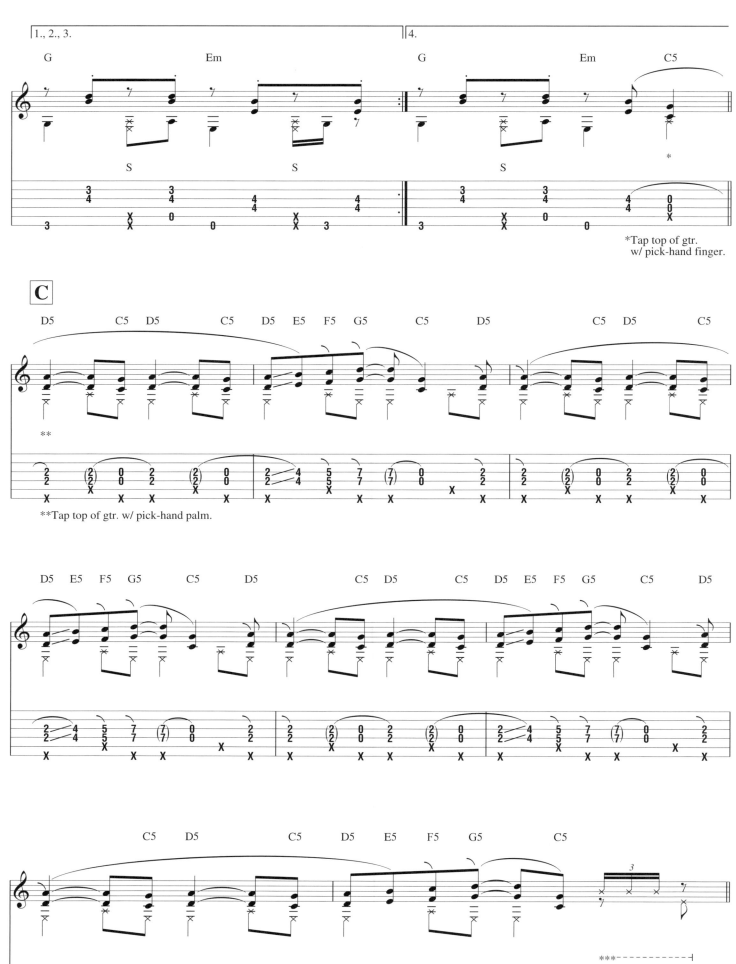

*Tap top of gtr.
 w/ pick-hand finger.

**Tap top of gtr. w/ pick-hand palm.

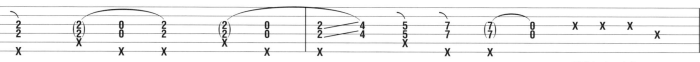

***As in pickup meas.

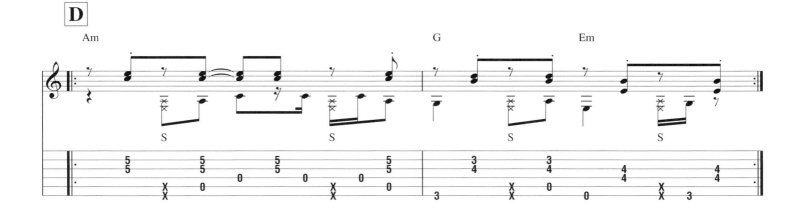

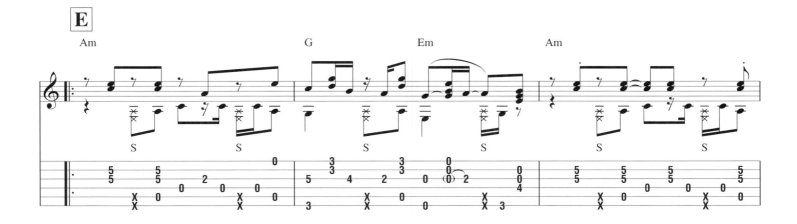

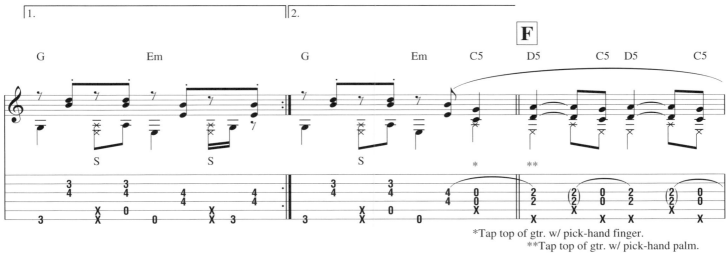

*Tap top of gtr. w/ pick-hand finger.
**Tap top of gtr. w/ pick-hand palm.

Play 6 times & fade

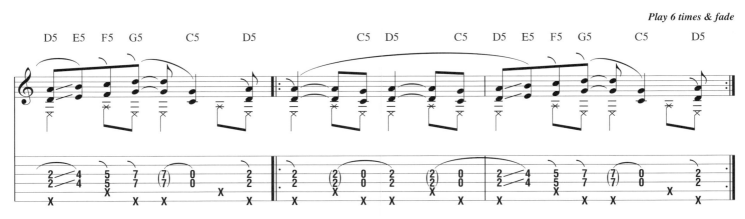

from Pete Huttlinger - *Fingerpicking Wonder*

Superstition

Words and Music by Stevie Wonder

Tune down 1/2 step:
(low to high) E♭-A♭-D♭-G♭-B♭-E♭

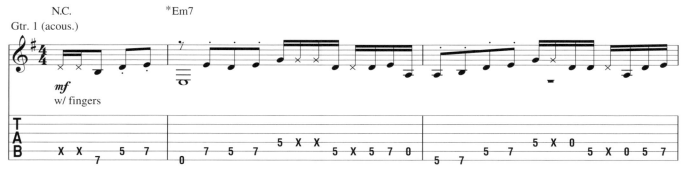

*Chord symbols reflect implied harmony.

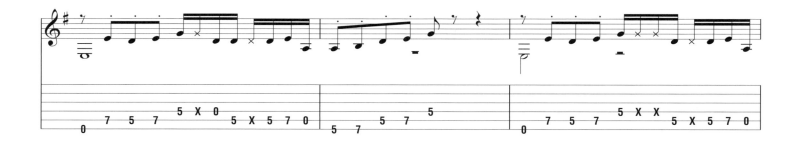

© 1972 (Renewed 2000) JOBETE MUSIC CO., INC. and BLACK BULL MUSIC
c/o EMI APRIL MUSIC INC.
This arrangement © 2013 JOBETE MUSIC CO., INC. and BLACK BULL MUSIC
c/o EMI APRIL MUSIC INC.
All Rights Reserved   International Copyright Secured   Used by Permission

2nd time, Gtr. 1: w/ Fill 1

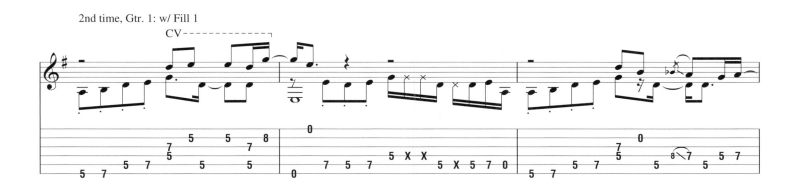

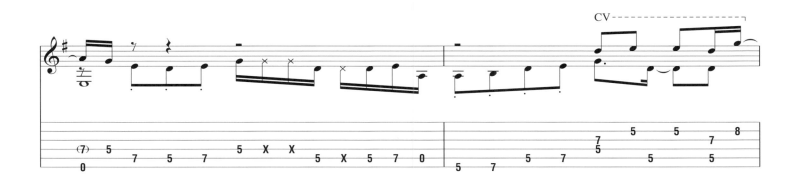

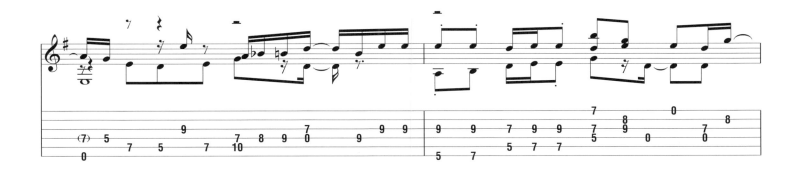

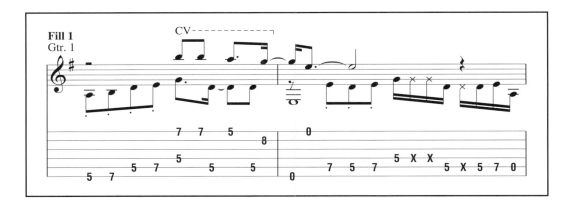

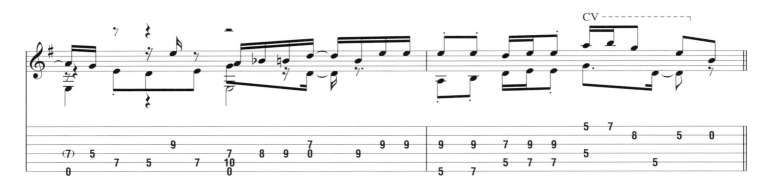

C

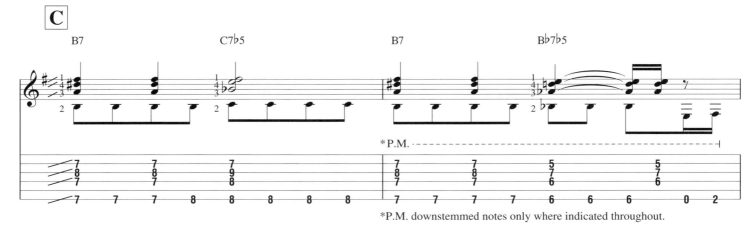

*P.M. downstemmed notes only where indicated throughout.

D

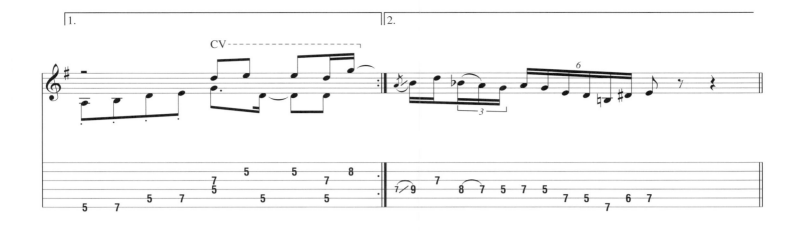

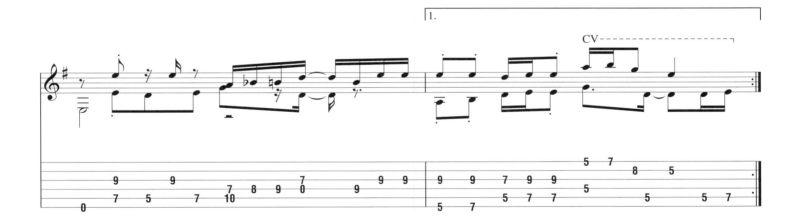

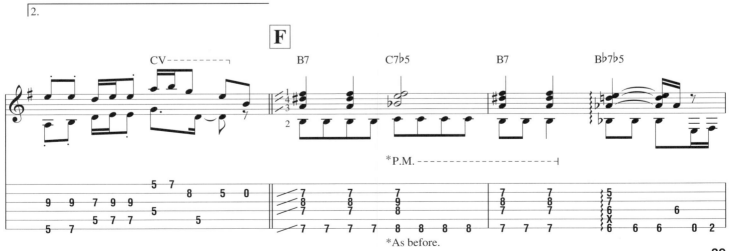

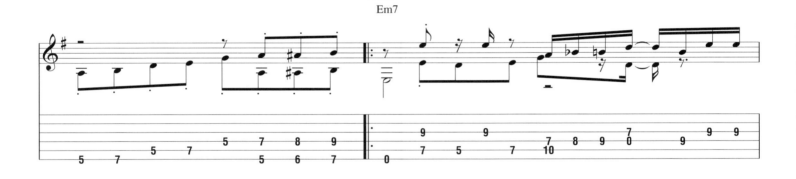

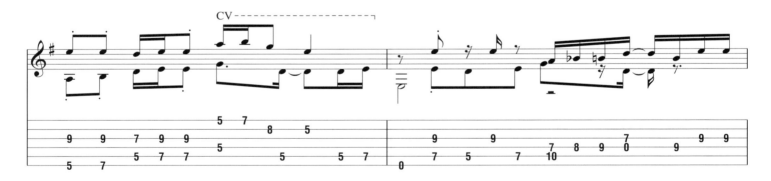

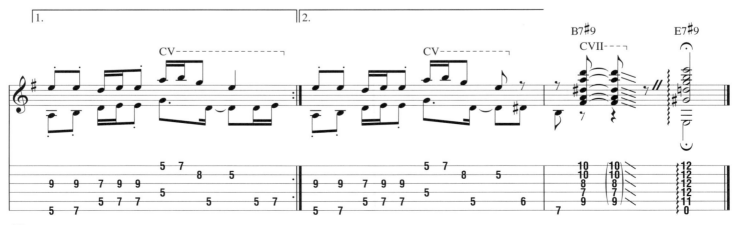

from Stephen Bennett - *In-A-Gadda-Da-Stephen*

A Whiter Shade of Pale

Words and Music by Keith Reid, Gary Brooker and Matthew Fisher

Drop D tuning:
(low to high) D-A-D-G-B-E

A

Moderately slow ♩ = 82

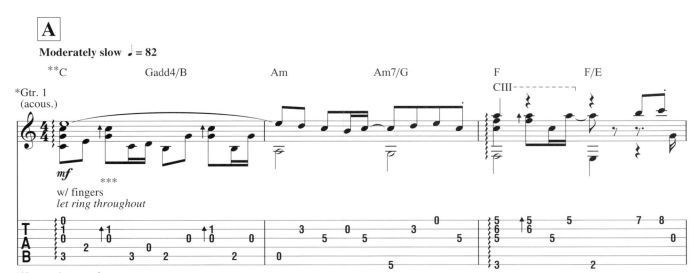

*Harp guitar arr. for gtr.
**Chord symbols reflect implpied harmony.
***Strike with back of pick-hand nails.

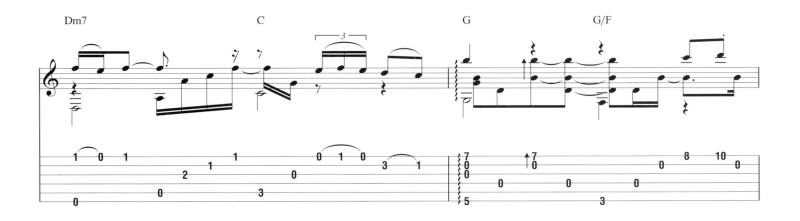

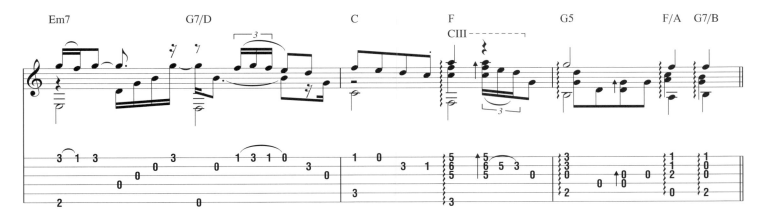

© Copyright 1967 (Renewed) Onward Music Ltd., London, England
TRO - Essex Music, Inc., New York, controls all publication rights for the U.S.A. and Canada
This arrangement TRO - © Copyright 2013 Essex Music, Inc.
International Copyright Secured
All Rights Reserved Including Public Performance For Profit
Used by Permission

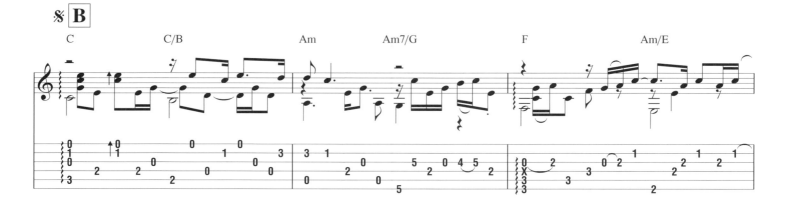

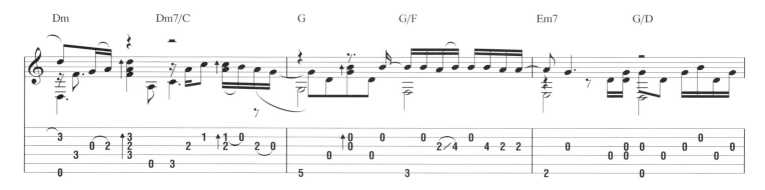

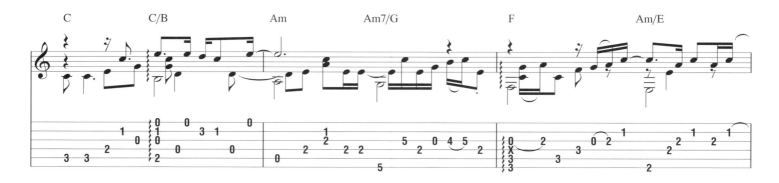

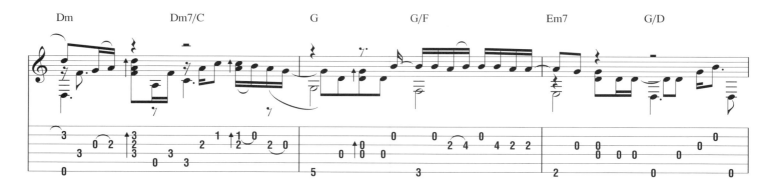

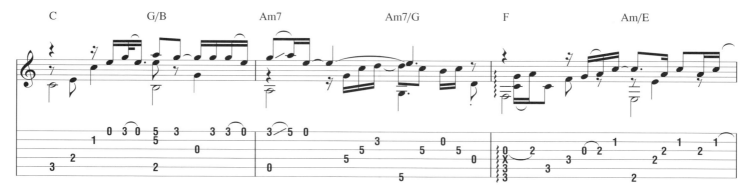

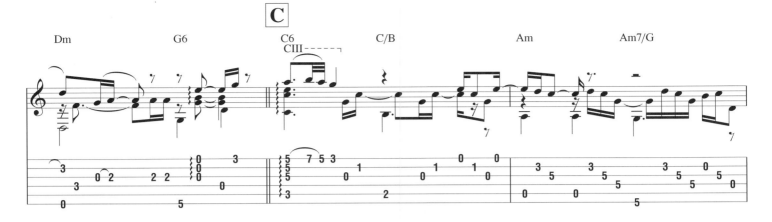

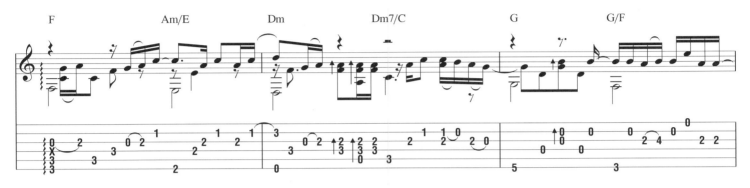

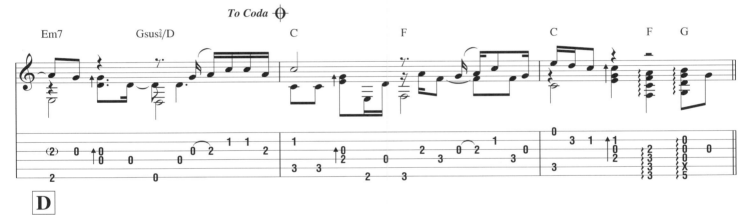

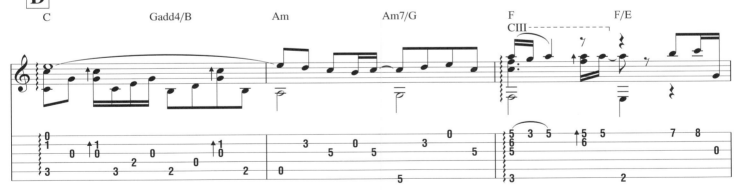

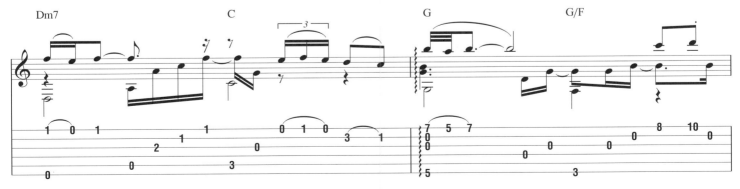

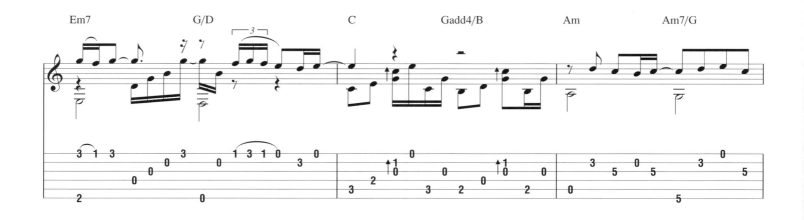

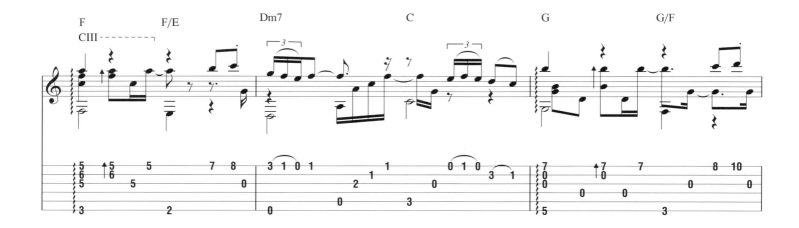

D.S. al Coda

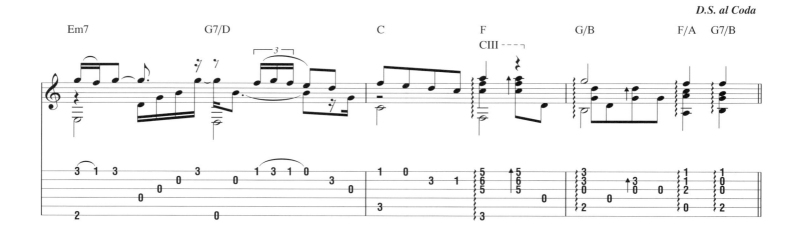

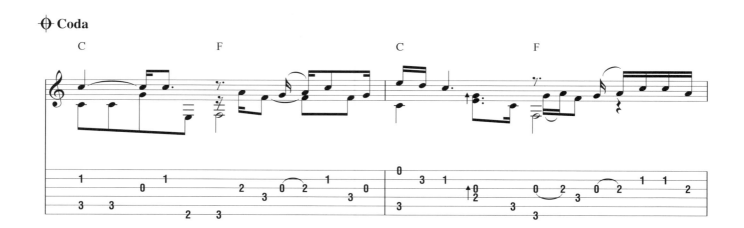

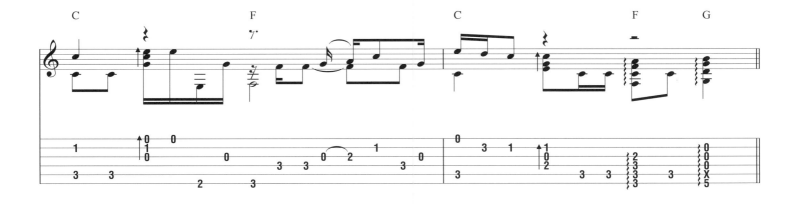

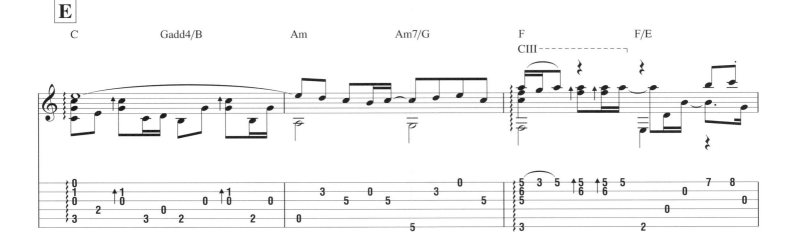

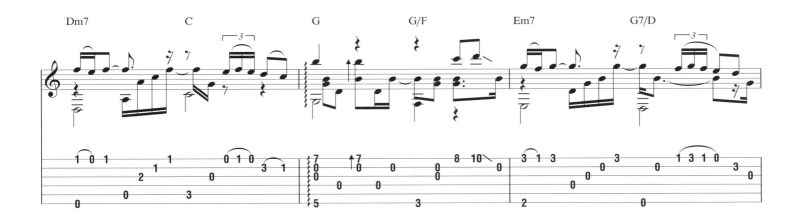

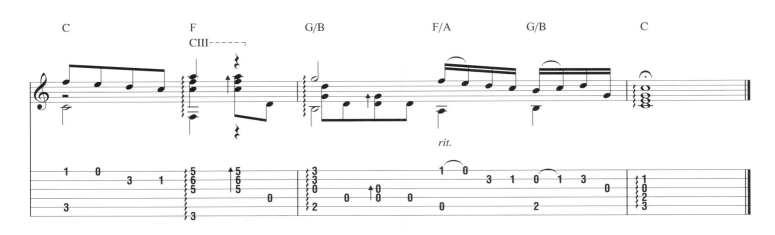

GUITAR NOTATION LEGEND

Guitar music can be notated three different ways: on a *musical staff*, in *tablature*, and in *rhythm slashes*.

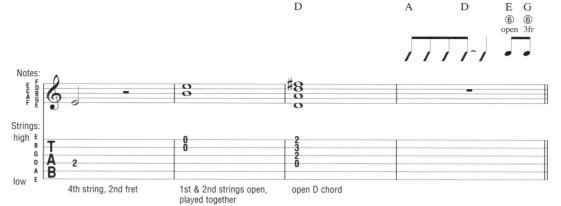

RHYTHM SLASHES are written above the staff. Strum chords in the rhythm indicated. Use the chord diagrams found at the top of the first page of the transcription for the appropriate chord voicings. Round noteheads indicate single notes.

THE MUSICAL STAFF shows pitches and rhythms and is divided by bar lines into measures. Pitches are named after the first seven letters of the alphabet.

TABLATURE graphically represents the guitar fingerboard. Each horizontal line represents a string, and each number represents a fret.

4th string, 2nd fret   1st & 2nd strings open, played together   open D chord

---

HALF-STEP BEND: Strike the note and bend up 1/2 step.

WHOLE-STEP BEND: Strike the note and bend up one step.

GRACE NOTE BEND: Strike the note and immediately bend up as indicated.

SLIGHT (MICROTONE) BEND: Strike the note and bend up 1/4 step.

BEND AND RELEASE: Strike the note and bend up as indicated, then release back to the original note. Only the first note is struck.

PRE-BEND: Bend the note as indicated, then strike it.

VIBRATO: The string is vibrated by rapidly bending and releasing the note with the fretting hand.

WIDE VIBRATO: The pitch is varied to a greater degree by vibrating with the fretting hand.

HAMMER-ON: Strike the first (lower) note with one finger, then sound the higher note (on the same string) with another finger by fretting it without picking.

PULL-OFF: Place both fingers on the notes to be sounded. Strike the first note and without picking, pull the finger off to sound the second (lower) note.

LEGATO SLIDE: Strike the first note and then slide the same fret-hand finger up or down to the second note. The second note is not struck.

SHIFT SLIDE: Same as legato slide, except the second note is struck.

TRILL: Very rapidly alternate between the notes indicated by continuously hammering on and pulling off.

TAPPING: Hammer ("tap") the fret indicated with the pick-hand index or middle finger and pull off to the note fretted by the fret hand.

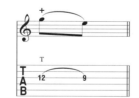

NATURAL HARMONIC: Strike the note while the fret-hand lightly touches the string directly over the fret indicated.

PINCH HARMONIC: The note is fretted normally and a harmonic is produced by adding the edge of the thumb or the tip of the index finger of the pick hand to the normal pick attack.

PICK SCRAPE: The edge of the pick is rubbed down (or up) the string, producing a scratchy sound.

MUFFLED STRINGS: A percussive sound is produced by laying the fret hand across the string(s) without depressing, and striking them with the pick hand.

PALM MUTING: The note is partially muted by the pick hand lightly touching the string(s) just before the bridge.

RAKE: Drag the pick across the strings indicated with a single motion.

TREMOLO PICKING: The note is picked as rapidly and continuously as possible.

VIBRATO BAR DIVE AND RETURN: The pitch of the note or chord is dropped a specified number of steps (in rhythm), then returned to the original pitch.

VIBRATO BAR SCOOP: Depress the bar just before striking the note, then quickly release the bar.

VIBRATO BAR DIP: Strike the note and then immediately drop a specified number of steps, then release back to the original pitch.

FINGERPICKING
GUITAR BOOKS

Hone your fingerpicking skills with these great songbooks featuring solo guitar arrangements in standard notation and tablature.
The arrangements in these books are carefully written for intermediate-level guitarists. Each song combines melody and harmony in
one superb guitar fingerpicking arrangement. Each book also includes an introduction to basic fingerstyle guitar.

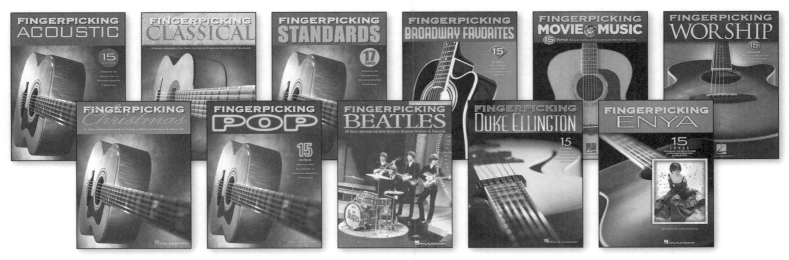

FINGERPICKING ACOUSTIC
00699614...$10.99

FINGERPICKING ACOUSTIC ROCK
00699764..$9.99

FINGERPICKING BACH
00699793..$8.95

FINGERPICKING BALLADS
00699717..$9.99

FINGERPICKING BEATLES
00699049..$19.99

FINGERPICKING BEETHOVEN
00702390..$7.99

FINGERPICKING BLUES
00701277 ....$7.99

FINGERPICKING BROADWAY FAVORITES
00699843..$9.99

FINGERPICKING BROADWAY HITS
00699838..$7.99

FINGERPICKING CELTIC FOLK
00701148..$7.99

FINGERPICKING CHILDREN'S SONGS
00699712..$9.99

FINGERPICKING CHRISTIAN
00701076 ....$7.99

FINGERPICKING CHRISTMAS
00699599..$8.95

FINGERPICKING CHRISTMAS CLASSICS
00701695..$7.99

FINGERPICKING CLASSICAL
00699620..$8.95

FINGERPICKING COUNTRY
00699687..$9.99

FINGERPICKING DISNEY
00699711..$10.99

FINGERPICKING DUKE ELLINGTON
00699845..$9.99

FINGERPICKING ENYA
00701161..$9.99

FINGERPICKING GOSPEL
00701059..$7.99

FINGERPICKING GUITAR BIBLE
00691040 ....$19.99

FINGERPICKING HYMNS
00699688..$8.95

FINGERPICKING IRISH SONGS
00701965..$7.99

FINGERPICKING JAZZ STANDARDS
00699840..$7.99

FINGERPICKING LATIN STANDARDS
00699837..$7.99

FINGERPICKING ANDREW LLOYD WEBBER
00699839..$9.99

FINGERPICKING LOVE SONGS
00699841..$9.99

FINGERPICKING LOVE STANDARDS
00699836 ....$9.99

FINGERPICKING LULLABYES
00701276..$9.99

FINGERPICKING MOVIE MUSIC
00699919..$9.99

FINGERPICKING MOZART
00699794..$8.95

FINGERPICKING POP
00699615..$9.99

FINGERPICKING PRAISE
00699714..$8.95

FINGERPICKING ROCK
00699716..$9.99

FINGERPICKING STANDARDS
00699613..$9.99

FINGERPICKING WEDDING
00699637..$9.99

FINGERPICKING WORSHIP
00700554..$7.99

**FINGERPICKING NEIL YOUNG –
GREATEST HITS**
00700134..$12.99

FINGERPICKING YULETIDE
00699654..$9.99

HAL•LEONARD®
CORPORATION
7777 W. BLUEMOUND RD. P.O. BOX 13819 MILWAUKEE, WI 53213

Visit Hal Leonard online at **www.halleonard.com**

Prices, contents and availability subject to change without notice.

STRUM IT GUITAR

AUTHENTIC CHORDS · ORIGINAL KEYS · COMPLETE SONGS

The *Strum It* series lets players strum the chords and sing along with their favorite hits. Each song has been selected because it can be played with regular open chords, barre chords, or other moveable chord types. Guitarists can simply play the rhythm, or play and sing along through the entire song. All songs are shown in their original keys complete with chords, strum patterns, melody and lyrics. Wherever possible, the chord voicings from the recorded versions are notated.

THE BEACH BOYS' GREATEST HITS
_____ 00699357......................................$12.95

THE BEATLES FAVORITES
_____ 00699249......................................$14.95

BEST OF CONTEMPORARY CHRISTIAN
_____ 00699531......................................$12.95

BEST OF STEVEN CURTIS CHAPMAN
_____ 00699530......................................$12.95

VERY BEST OF JOHNNY CASH
_____ 00699514......................................$14.99

CELTIC GUITAR SONGBOOK
_____ 00699265..$9.95

CHRISTMAS SONGS FOR GUITAR
_____ 00699247......................................$10.95

CHRISTMAS SONGS WITH 3 CHORDS
_____ 00699487..$8.95

VERY BEST OF ERIC CLAPTON
_____ 00699560......................................$12.95

COUNTRY STRUMMIN'
_____ 00699119..$8.95

JIM CROCE – CLASSIC HITS
_____ 00699269......................................$10.95

VERY BEST OF JOHN DENVER
_____ 00699488......................................$12.95

NEIL DIAMOND
_____ 00699593......................................$12.95

DISNEY FAVORITES
_____ 00699171......................................$10.95

BEST OF THE DOORS
_____ 00699177......................................$12.99

MELISSA ETHERIDGE GREATEST HITS
_____ 00699518......................................$12.99

FAVORITE SONGS WITH 3 CHORDS
_____ 00699112..$8.95

FAVORITE SONGS WITH 4 CHORDS
_____ 00699270..$8.95

FIRESIDE SING-ALONG
_____ 00699273..$8.95

FOLK FAVORITES
_____ 00699517..$8.95

IRVING BERLIN'S GOD BLESS AMERICA®
_____ 00699508..$9.95

GREAT '50s ROCK
_____ 00699187..$9.95

GREAT '60s ROCK
_____ 00699188..$9.95

GREAT '70s ROCK
_____ 00699262..$9.95

THE GUITAR STRUMMERS' ROCK SONGBOOK
_____ 00701678......................................$14.99

BEST OF WOODY GUTHRIE
_____ 00699496......................................$12.95

JOHN HIATT COLLECTION
_____ 00699398......................................$12.95

THE VERY BEST OF BOB MARLEY
_____ 00699524......................................$12.95

A MERRY CHRISTMAS SONGBOOK
_____ 00699211..$9.95

MORE FAVORITE SONGS WITH 3 CHORDS
_____ 00699532..$8.95

THE VERY BEST OF TOM PETTY
_____ 00699336......................................$12.95

POP-ROCK GUITAR FAVORITES
_____ 00699088..$8.95

ELVIS! GREATEST HITS
_____ 00699276......................................$10.95

BEST OF GEORGE STRAIT
_____ 00699235......................................$14.99

TAYLOR SWIFT FOR ACOUSTIC GUITAR
_____ 00109717......................................$16.99

BEST OF HANK WILLIAMS JR.
_____ 00699224......................................$12.95

HAL • LEONARD®
7777 W. BLUEMOUND RD. P.O. BOX 13819 MILWAUKEE, WI 53213

Visit Hal Leonard online at **www.halleonard.com**

Prices, contents & availability subject to change without notice.

0113